Memories of the Future

by

John F King

Isbn
978-0-9931306-7-0

York European Publishing
2019

www.johnkinginternational.co.uk

www.johnkinginternational.eu

Longcase clock, Spiegelhalter Whitby

'It makes sense to see memory as the other side of the future…'

Adventures in Memory: the Science and Secrets of Remembering and Forgetting.
H & Y Østby 2018

Introduction

There comes a point when you realise there is more time behind you than in front. Naturally you don't know exactly when this time is or what to do with the realisation. Is there a shape to it all, like a laying out a CV stacking up courses, to jobs to transferable skills or is it to misquote Twain, one thing after another?

The so-called Time plays of J B Priestley have plot lines that play on concepts of linear time, of what ifs, hope, promise, missed turnings, opportunities taken, a time when it is too late. Or is it?

It is never too late to start, to rethink, to do what you always wanted to do, to do something for the first time, to do something you always did for the last time.

The essential written pieces here derive from my completion of a course entitled *Writing Lives*, offered online through Oxford University in the Autumn of 2018.

The course encouraged us to think not only conceptually and ethically about life writing and memoir but also dramatically. Why and how can your life be of interest to others, can you know the pivots of a life when you are living through them or through hindsight?

'…that eternal question of what constitutes experience? A close examination of what happened at any given period in itself provokes an unnatural element, like looking at a large oil painting under a magnifying glass, the over-all effect lost.'

Anthony Powell: *Temporary Kings*

In *Brief Answers to the Big Questions* Professor Hawking speculates 'it is a matter of common experience that things get more disordered and chaotic with time…'

You simply did the best you could with the information you had available at the time. You intended not to hurt people on the way, if you did you tried to say sorry and promise never to do it again. After all, you're older now, aren't you?

Contents

Introduction

Vienna – Leeds

About a Buoy

Cynthetic

'Afternoon Men'

Keith wouldn't like it

Last Bus

By Pass

C is for Collegiate

Capital Code

4-sided bay

The deed is done

Relativity

Check Off

F is for Fortitude

Live in Leeds

Different Trains

Time line

Vienna – Leeds, single or return

Place. What could be more important? Watching Jools Holland's TV music programme on New Year Eve every band is introduced by where they are from, on quiz programme *University Challenge Christmas Special* each student says 'my name is – I am from –.' It is the first thing we know about them. This is usually, though not always, the place where they were born. In music a place may become sonically synonymous - a Viennese Waltz, the Viennese school.

My name is John King. I am from Leeds. Simple. Isn't it? Yes and no. If you are Second Generation then where was your first generation from? Have you been (back) there in reality or imagination, or both? Do you need to? When? How?

I left Leeds by train in 1975. It seems a long time ago now in place, in time, in sound. The destination? Leeds. My InterRail ticket would bring me back in a month to where I started but there may be changes in between. I still have my passbook, now not a valid ticket but part of an autobiography. In 1975 I didn't have a concept of being Second Generation, I hadn't arrived there yet, the journey was only beginning.

The trains ran night and day, London Paris Nice, Milan, Geneva, Vienna Budapest Vienna – again, a hindsight coincidence? (I learned the German for hindsight then) – through the night to Hamburg, Copenhagen, Stockholm, Luleå, Oslo, on through Germany, Ostend, London.

Vienna then to me was not as I may think of it now the birthplace of my mother (26 August 1928) .

It was significant to me as it describes itself (www.wien.info): a city of music. I walked and trammed through the city of Beethoven, Berg, Haydn, Lehár, Mozart, Schubert, Schönberg, Strauss, Zemlinsky.

This was the home of the *Musikverein*, the concert hall we saw on the TV in our house in Leeds every new years day. At the statues of the musicians I had my picture taken on the Olympus SLR camera my Dad had given me for the journey. The film was later to be lost at another stage of my journey when I inadvertently opened the camera case in the glaring Alpine sun.

Mozart Statue, Vienna.

On my return to Leeds my mother asked me about my grand European tour. There was no specific mention of Vienna.

I unpacked my rucksack of memories, refilled it with books and returned to Leeds station for the train to University.

My Dad waved me off on the station platform. Years later I returned again to the now recession hit city and began an unsuccessful quest for work. It was some time before I saw an advertisement for work in the civil service. The form required me to fill in details of my family on both sides going as far back as my grandparents.

To my surprise my Dad was reluctant to help me complete the form. I eventually came to understand it as he saw it — he wanted to protect my mother.

Reading many articles in *Voices* I have often noted how other Second Generation writers describe their awareness of unexplained silences, gaps, otherness, apartness, things not quite adding up.

I recalled as a child some of the comparatively exotic dishes my mother cooked, the 'relatives' who came to stay with us from Mannheim and Mainz called Helga or Waldemar, the time my mother inexplicably left in the middle of a family holiday in Sussex to go to a funeral in Brussels of more relatives I didn't know we had, the 'Viennese' piano music that wafted up the stairs as my mother played the Scheidmayer piano. A friend commented on the accented V sound in my mother's English. I couldn't hear it. Perhaps being from Leeds wasn't all that simple.

 / *Our family donated our piano to Opera North, Leeds Grand Theatre 2011 in memory of my mother and musical associations with Leeds.*

/My mother's postcard from Brussels

My mother, Elsie, had never said to me ' John, my original name was Ilse, I'm from Vienna'

The first time I knew this as a fact was when my Dad finally gave me the completed form for the civil service.

Mother's birth name: Ilse Hölzelmacher

Birthplace: Vienna

The form eventually led me to employment in the Foreign Office library and to Chatham House, where my responsibilities included researching European politics. I began too, from this departure point to increase my own research, my own connection to the bigger picture of political history on our continent, a history, like the music to which I felt a connection.

I called up an article from Chatham House library, the headline in *The Independent* dateline 9 July 1991: ' Austria faces its past.'

With the information my dad had given me for my form I wrote to the Austrian Embassy in London who forwarded my inquiry to the Israelitische Kultusgemeinde in Vienna.

By November (of course this is decades before online research instruments and the ITS techniques recently the subject of a Second Generation Network meeting) I received a written reply from the Attaché of the Austrian Embassy London with the sentence:

'I hope the following information can suit your requirements'-

Alfons Hölzelmacher, born 8 November 1930 last address Wien II, Mohapelgasse (nowadays Tempelgasse) deported to Theresienstadt 25 February 1943 and to Auschwitz 23 October 1944

Hilde Hölzelmacher born 2 November 1881, last address Wien I, Kai 39 deported to Ghetto Riga 11 January 1942

Sali Hölzelmacher born 25 January 1867, last address Wien I, Lazenhof was deported to Theresienstadt 5 January 1943.

I have never been to Vienna with this information. My mother told me of a holiday she and her husband Terence enjoyed in Austria, a holiday of air, scenery and music. As she grew older I asked her to talk more of her childhood in Vienna, a childhood that seemed quite happy, of learning piano and clarinet at her school in Ruprechtstrasse, the Vienna she left behind on the Kindertransport of 1939.

I asked her more of her life in Vienna but desisted seeing the trauma it caused her. Shortly before she died, in Leeds, she told me 'I think of Alfons every day.'

Every Holocaust Memorial Day I light a candle for him, and all the family, and of course all those lost in the darkness.

Vienna is still the city of music. Equally so is Leeds, where I was born and grew up listening to music, though on the last census form, which I filled in by myself, when asked to tick the box where I was from I marked 'other' and wrote in the blank white box ' British European'.

Article from **Second Generation Voices** *2017*

www.secondgeneration.org.uk

/ *Original Photograph: Elsie and Terence, 1951*

About a Buoy

Looking back I'm glad I was kind to him at the time.

Not later, retrospective respect but in the now.

Standing at the school gates in his Navy uniform he seemed in the right place.

Back then you could leave school at 14. Percy, all at sea at school, simply sailed away.

He wasn't the brightest boy – some of our less enlightened brethren used his name, plank, and other words in the same sentence.

He wasn't aloof, self-contained, a self-appointed loner, he was lonely, lost, isolated. I never knew why, who, including him, could be responsible. Do people chose to be alone. Really?

On his last day I saw him cast away, that defeated walk of his. There were not many waves for Percy.

It was three years before anyone heard of him again, but to be direct not that many were listening on his wavelength. It was my last day by that time too. There was a cluster around the gates. He wasn't that tall but stood up straight, passing his white hat on for people to try on. Polaroids emerged and to cap it all, flares were in.

abctales

Cynthetic

'Bradford 2570126.'

She is the only person I know who answers the telephone like that.

'Cynth, it's Terry. Fancy a trip to the theatre next week? *Look Back in Anger.*'

'Sorry?'

'The play. *Look Back in Anger.*''

'I haven't read the reviews yet.'

The play reached the end of the season before we spoke again. I mean before I rang her.

'Bradford 2570126.'

'Hey, Cynth, you missed a cracking production there.'

'I'm sorry?'

'*Look Back in Anger.*''

 How apt might have been a classy response but…

'Listen Cynth, I thought we might try that Portuguese restaurant..'

'I haven't read the reviews yet.'

'Let me get back to you.'

I never met anyone who answers the phone like Cynthia.

'Afternoon Men'

The house was never renovated.

It was the same the day we bought it as that day I, being the last to leave, closed the door and never went back.

It wasn't the foremost feature, probably the priority was relatively low but one reason my Dad liked the house was he could come home for lunch.

I don't think that many engineers at manufacturing plants came home during the day, even for forty minutes.

We had all our meals in the kitchen. The centre of this room was the boiler. This came alive according to the thermostat, seasonally adjusted. The noise from the boiler filled Winter silences, punctuated Spring conversations, whooshed along with Autumn reflections. I wasn't there in summers.

Next to the boiler was my Dad's chair. It was a deckchair. I liked the way he sat there after lunch, a post prandial cigarette before returning to the factory to make things. Sometimes he looked out in front of him as if staring out to sea or competed with the boiler with stories of machines being made to be exported across the globe.

It was all perfectly calibrated, home, lunch, cig, back. 10 minutes each way in the Morris.

Then came the lunch when he never went back. In fact he didn't have the lunch just the cigarette.

I knew something was wrong with the world the way he came into the kitchen that day. I heard the car draw up in the drive, he walked in but didn't make it past the boiler to the kitchen table.

The smoke was rising from the deckchair.

'Everything cool, Dad?' I said. I wasn't long back from University, I wasn't studying engineering.

He lit another cigarette. It was 1250. This was serious. He should have had the salad, he should be back in the Morris, he should…

'Everything alright, Dad?' I said

'It's over,' he said.

The boiler shuddered. He'd clarify in his own time.

'25 years. It's over. I suppose I had a good run.'

It wasn't an expression – a good run – I would use. It was one of his expressions and this was about him.

The deck chair seemed to have enveloped him, I wondered if he'd ever get up again, if the sea would rise into the kitchen.

'Doors close, doors open, Dad,' I said. He looked at me. He had spent more years at the factory than I had on the planet.

I modified my approach. 'I thought you said the order books were full. That new supersonic jet for the RAF, locomotives for the Indian Railways.'

'Automation.'

'Automation?'

'Entire draughtsmen's department. Gone.'

I have never seen a man so defeated. This was my Dad. He had to get up, pack up the deckchair, create the post-industrial life.

The world was never the same again. Retirement so obviously hadn't worked out, a transition unattained.

It was only three years later when I returned to clear the house. I looked through old photographs. Where was it, Interlaken, Zermatt? Somewhere like that. In the background there were people skiing, sports clothes covered in logos, white teeth. In the foreground, Dad in his tweed winter coat, flat cap. He used to criticise me for not smiling in photographs. I let this one pass.

I don't know where that photograph is now.

The boiler was too silent to comment. It must have been late Spring. I folded up the deckchair and walked into the garden.

The engineering plant at Bradford/ the bus was an option if the Morris 1800 overheated /

Keith Wouldn't Like It

'How do you know, has he ever said anything to you, I mean really?'

It wasn't the first comment on the subject and probably not the last.

Few jokes stand repetition, especially those that are merely marginally funny the first time and are on me.

I don't talk about them as much as I used to – Keith, Charlie, Mick, Ronnie – time isn't on my side. One needs to keep moving forward, music , tastes, technology, whatever.

I first heard them in that centre of world music – Leeds. Mid 1970s. Their founder member, who I was never on first terms with, left, fired or to use retro terminology, let go. He was replaced by a man who I totally rated – Taylor.

It was the summer before the mock A/S levels, but a time when I never did 'mocking.' I hope I never have.

I came across a troupe of travelling players in Leeds, Armley, amongst the terraced houses not yet demolished. I never attached any significance to the genealogical fact that Armley was the district of Leeds I was born in. I was into what they, *Interplay*, did: musical street theatre. Among their number was a latter day minstrel equally proficient on guitar or piano. The guitar was wiser for the street. We called Ian the human jukebox. Call out any song, he would play it.

'Got any Stones?' sounded a catch phrase of the period, for me it was to become a catch phrase of any period. Ian said ' watch this' in his North Leeds / South London vernacular and launched into *Jumpin' Jack Flash*. I've always looked back.

/Agony Column, the Interplay house band.

Things were not going too well musically speaking at the Yorkshire College of Music. It was a time of life, 16, 17, when the time of the day and week were not in sync with the time signature of Brahms *Piano Variations* op24. I had no talent, if the application went I would have nothing.

It took two buses to travel there, or one if I took the West Yorkshire 670 and walked up the Kirkstall Hill, from the abbey, past Headingley cricket ground to the college.

Piano teacher Miss W believed, with foundation, I was the weakest link in the yearly concert programme of her students.

Why the Brahms was selected is a mystery I haven't invested time in solving. Even before other musical and non-musical influences were overwhelming me Brahms wasn't up there. Chopin, yes, Holst, Richard Strauss, right, but have you seen the time and key signatures on this?

Miss W's technique was old school. Decompose a piece into micro sections, work on it bar by bar, build it back up. Parts make a whole. Phrasing, emphasis, tone. It wasn't coming together. Quite the opposite. Someone would break first, she read correctly it wouldn't be Brahms.

'What do you listen to in your spare time?' she asked. I was about to say what spare time but realised she was doing me a favour.

'The Rolling Stones,' I said. I've always aspired to honesty in music, I don't only say what people want to hear.

'That would explain everything,' said Miss W, not missing a beat, then stared at the Bösendorfer for the equivalent of four bars of the Brahms before saying 'bring something in next week, we'll analyse it.'

I walked up Kirkstall Hill the following Friday with *Sticky Fingers* under my arm. It was *de rigueur* for boys – men – of my age in that time to stroll about town with LP covers accidentally facing out. Rolling Stones, Soft Machine, Miles Davis, Floyd all seemed to have LP sleeve designs issued with mega capital letters proclaiming Look at Me.

I cleared the Abbado, Arrau, Karajan and placed the vinyl on the turntable next to Bösendorfer.

'What is this track called?' inquired W.

I supplied the information: *'Can't you Hear me Knocking?'* Neither of us smiled.

Taylor had recently joined the Stones line up and gave them this new, spacy, jazzy sound. The track is mainly instrumental and progresses through major / minor key modulations. Miss W and I could analyse them.

I thought she might say why do you like it, which would be more difficult to analyse. When Keith Richards and Taylor struck the final G7/9 chord she said 'and the Brahms?'

Fortunately I looked older than my years then - I repaired to the Original Oak for a *Tuborg*.

It was years later when I was disembarking from a number 11 bus at the Worlds End end of Kings Road when I heard the sound again.

I thought I might have died but I was only in my mid-twenties. The unmistakeable sound, the unhurried space between notes, a blend of rock and blues without being lost to either.

The Stones and I had gone through some line-up changes but were basically the same. As ever I followed the sound. Upstairs in a pub there was a group of men in some ways as ordinary as me. In appearance. The sound was amazing, ringing out in space and time.

I have not been in many pubs when the police have been called. True, music this good may be barely legal. Noise is not the word I would use here but the PC saw it as his duty. Mr Taylor was allowed to continue as long as the windows were closed. It was a hot evening.

I had seen a Stone, I have never seen the Stones. Why? Time, money, place, logistics, chance or deliberation. Excuses? Would realisation be a qualified disappointment, something best left alone like a Lords Test match or an east west train journey across the United States seated in the observation car.

Has the moment has passed, it's better this way, you can't always get what you want?

I haven't always worn plain T-shirts, perhaps logoed T-shirts are the late middle-aged man's equivalent of the teenager's non-covered LP covers.

When my nieces were old enough to read they asked me about the logos. Uncle John, who or what are the Rolling Stones? I deciphered for them. They continued with what they were doing. When they were old enough to go to concerts they asked me with characteristic kindness - I'll get tickets to the O2 show for us. If you have a chance to rectify a situation before it is too late you should do it.

Was there a situation to be rectified? Everything was alright as it was.

Don't worry about me I said, I'll listen on the iPlayer.

Keith wouldn't like it.

Interplay Archive Project
www.unfinishedhistories.com

The Rolling Stones played in Richmond 1962 - .

I enjoyed spring strolls on Richmond Hill terrace when I lived in Richmond in the 1980s.

Rolling Stones, fifth Ave, NYC 1975 painting by R Wood who succeeded Taylor.
I visited NYC , NY state by air and rail 1989

Memories of the Future
ISBN 9780993130670

Last Bus

'Would you like to come r*a*spberry picking with us?'

I never knew an ' a ' could be so long. I was off balance for 7 seconds. Any longer and I was going to look rude and first impressions can't be over turned after that amount of time. I finally came up with an answer that didn't have an '*a*' in it. I could expand on it later if it was politic.

'Yeh, nice.' I said.

Calverley in the mid-1970s was still a village. Six miles north west of Leeds and you could walk a few yards to the raspberry lane. It was the best suburb of Leeds I'd ever lived in. Pudsey, where we had that month moved from was not only on the other side of the city it was on another planet. I had a good time there, watching the cricket at the St Lawrence club, pulling levers on an old steam engine permanently parked near the market square but that was childhood. Do you want that to go on forever? Pick the fruit.

I went raspberry picking with the doctor's son and bell ringing with the wing commander's daughter. I hadn't the mind space to check how my vocabulary sounded, it was more fun to expand it.

Mum and Dad had pushed themselves to the financial limit to buy the house. The stone-built end of terrace opposite Calverley Old Hall was on the market for a solar system stretching £55K. My parents put the financial package together by every legal means possible. It wasn't enough. The estate agent gazumped us. Dad non-bluffed his offer was final. The owners told the estate agent 'we're Quakers.'

Church of St Wilfred, Calverley

Everything was peachy. There was only one thorn to life in Calverley Hills. The last bus.

On Spring evenings I set out to explore the cultural life of mid1970s Leeds and Bradford. The Halle Orchestra at Bradford's St Georges Hall programmed their rep of overture (*Egmont*) new work (Lutoslawski), classic (Haydn) perfectly.

As a sixth former at Cardinal Hinsley Grammar School, Bradford I attended the Halle subscription concerts, 1974, 1975

Even Jimmy Porter couldn't complain that curtain down at Bradford Playhouse's production of *Look Back in Anger* was 10pm. It was in the increasingly cosmopolitan Leeds that the issue was becoming most apparent.

Generally I sailed into Leeds on the top deck of the West Yorkshire bus services 670 at 6.20pm. Two Peter Stuyvesants later - I smoked the extra length at that period - I'd disembark on the Headrow in central Leeds. The choices here were as splendid as the adjacent Town Hall. My top group of the era, Soft Machine were touring here with their extended *fifth* album, a purely instrumental virtuosic performance.

I ran for the last bus before they were playing side two.

The following year, touring with their epic *Six* album their timing was perfect. Mine wasn't.

I saw the receding red lights of the red bus. I walked six miles, the mist or dew coating the ring road as I dreamed of future life in an inner-city apartment.

The walk invigorated my thinking – was this music and theatre autodidactic worth it? In the film world my exposure to Antonioni was more challenging.

It was now the second time I'd bussed and walked to the Continental film evenings at Leeds Playhouse determined to complete *Blow Up*. On the previous outing photographer David Hemmings was developing the film frames in the studio – had he unwittingly captured a corpse? I stayed to the limit on the second viewing, but the photos were still unformed in the tray with the red light on. I only made the bus with seconds.

'Good evening, young man?' inquired the conductor as he clipped through the smog of the upper deck.

I made no comment, I realised he didn't direct timetables.

The third showing would have to be final. The taxi fare was murder.

The original Leeds Playhouse of the 1970s/

/ rebuilt in Leeds Cultural Quarter 2019.

I supported the redevelopment scheme 'Sit with Us' as a patron to mark the plays, films, music, events I have attended there.

My play Loop *was given a read through by members of the WYP company in association with Sound Stage North and Script Yorkshire, 2004.*

Leeds town hall, music venue from the Orchestra of Opera North to Soft Machine

Memories of the Future

York Europe Publishing

JK
2019

By Pass

When I first made the journey it took two days.

My father drove the Ford Thames from Yorkshire to Cornwall, Leeds to Hayle.

I sat in the front seat, an honorary navigator. I knew he knew the way. He was my Dad.

It was pre-motorway, pre satnav, pre a lot of stuff. There wasn't enough to bypass. We drove through the centre of cities, towns, villages. There was so much to discover. The industrial north turned green, the grey sea blue.

'One day you will make journeys on your own, bigger cities, bluer seas, overseas. ' my Dad said to me.

The van engine was situated between us, humming warmly day one, hot and clanky day two. I think it was glad to rest when we finally parked on the grass in front of Uncle Henry's farm. Uncle Henry came out to greet us.

'Welcome, young man,' he said, his voice unplaceable, melodic, a kindly tone. I'd never met a farmer before.

Over the spring days he showed us round, he kept pigs and hens, organic. His wife Isobel looked after the flower side of the business. They helped me help them – planting, cattle feeding, hedge clearing. Nice work.

When the van recovered we went even further, as far as sea and tides permitted. St Michaels Mount. Lands End.

Two years later we made the journey again. One day. Train. This time I travelled with my mum and sister. Dad stayed home working overtime. We were on one train all day but had a compartment to ourselves. I looked out of the window as the train skimmed the coastline.

By now it was a different season. The jobs varied: hay bales, picking fruit that hadn't yet fallen.

I waved good bye to Auntie Isobel and Uncle Henry on the station platform. I was never to see them again.

Dad was right. I've been on virtually every continent except Antarctica. Maybe it will melt and come to me.

I wouldn't say I've been back to Cornwall. I'd say I've been again. 6 hours. VW. No maps.

It's taken a long time to get there that quickly. The cities we went through are signposted from the motorway but we never go there.

They've all gone now, Dad, Mum, sister, Henry, Isobel, the boy who waved goodbye.

Michaelmas 2018

On the south west coastal path 2017. ADL

The mainline from Yorkshire / London to Devon / Cornwall.

Arrival and departure, Fowey, 2017. ADL

C is for Collegiate

'Direct ticket or via London?'

Looking back from now would I have changed my route?

'Direct,' I replied.

The train journey from Leeds to Oxford is not express in speed. It is in visuals, loaded with freight.

I pulled down the carriage window cord and signalled to my Dad, receding on Leeds station platform. Neither of us will ever know if the other cried.

I hope I remember correctly that I thanked him before the diesel engine curtailed formalities.

The train curved through the industrial goneness of mid 70s south Leeds. It is some time before the landscape turns green. The reflections in the train window are too strong to read any book. Past the crooked spire of that Midlands church, the bombed remains of a pub in Birmingham, riding past Banbury Cross before straight spires are visible across meadows.

The diesel leaves me on another platform. My father isn't there. I walk with my suitcase from the station to the city centre. This part of the city is indistinguishable from any other, traffic islands overrun by products of British Leyland, chain stores of remaindered flares.

Then it becomes different. The buildings of unblackened stone, church-like even when they aren't.

I haul my wheel-less suitcase along the quad until I see a staircase with my name sign on it. That never happened before. Or since.

At dinner men who were boys a year ago enunciate grace in Latin.

'How you doing, man?'

It is after dinner in the quad, a young man with curls and Levi's offers me a Rothmans. I think it might help my digestion although the meal was barely edible.

I will always remember his smile, even when it was unbalanced by a stroke 40 years later.

He was the first to speak to me or the first to speak a language I could understand.

It was an Autumn evening. We drank Morrells bitter outside the Kings Arms. Sometimes you don't have to say much to know people. I felt I had known C for a long time. It must have been hours. He was from Richmond, the Surrey one, I was from Leeds. Apart from the North South equation there was nothing to divide us.

My circle of acquaintances gradually expanded but I always loved that south west London charm, the self-effacement of a young man who knew more than I did about things I didn't there was anything to know about.

'I am certain you are going to fail,' said Miss Waldstein.

She didn't have a sign on her North Oxford staircase so how was I to know she had a PhD? Miss - I don't feel like awarding her a doctorate - Waldstein's job was to tutor history undergraduates in the German texts to a level where they could pass the part one examination at the end of the first term. I wasn't sure if her diagnostic was a sign of expertise. If I failed was she a failure too because she wouldn't help me to pass or a success because she had a facility for prediction?

It was all academic. I survived the exam, it would soon be Christmas. With the grant money I saved in withholding Miss Waldstein's Weinachten present I bought my Dad a bottle of the college Port. The college arms adorned the bottle.

At home in Yorkshire Dad correctly circulated the Port with the Wensleydale and Stilton cheeses.

I had journeyed home the same way I had set off. I don't think I had changed that much apart from setting the priest an escape proof syllogism trap at the end of midnight mass. It was the sort of thing I did then. I don't know who's benefit it was intended for.

Snow was falling as we emerged from St Joseph's, the priest's faith unshaken.

'C is in his office,' said his mum on the telephone.

'Office?' I said. I was at Kings Cross station, direct train, Leeds to London.

It was the first vacation, first time on my own in London. I ran out of coins for the telephone. The pips were timing me out.

'Orange Tree, Richmond,' C's mum said. I went there directly.

Life before mobile phones, Internet, email was texturally different.

C was in the Orange Tree. I saw him instantly, he'd just come out of the pub phone booth, pint in one hand, Rothman's in the other.

'What's happening, man?' I said, 'Your mum said you were in your office.'

'Like it?' he smiled, making a sweeping gesture around the pub.

Richmond remains my favourite London village. It was the best university vacation ever.

Back in Oxford, work, friendships, life was moving forward. That is until it stopped. Forty years later I still analyse it.

The history course for the first year was demanding but what I wanted. But then it wasn't. I couldn't do it any more, compose essays on Kings and Queens, civil war, medieval courts. What was the point? For something that started so well the ending was so abrupt. There were no maps for this. The journey was over.

The communication came by note, alphabetically left in the college mail boxes known as pigeon holes. Perhaps it was a fitting way to be summoned.

'We need to talk. It is overdue. Please arrange to come to my study at your earliest convenience.'

The polite imperative wasn't lost on me, lost as I was.

The don's study was at the front of the college. From the window opposite Tom Tower Christ Church was visible. It had been there 450 years longer than me.

The room was full of books, most of which he had written.

'This conversation is long overdue,' said the Don, 'would you care to explain what is happening?' I had been there long enough to understand 'would you care' constructions. I told him the truth. The course – his course – wasn't what I wanted anymore, I couldn't continue, I had no motivation, I had reached an impasse. I would have to leave, go somewhere else, start anew.

He seemed to take centuries to absorb this. The bells of the tower begun to toll. When they stopped he spoke.

'You could just coast to the end.'

I was almost half way through the degree. I excelled exam requirements, my essays were good, it was only I couldn't do it anymore.

I can still hear his words now. It was exactly the wrong thing to say to me. I was twenty years old. Coasting was inadmissible, unattractive, dishonourable.

'I don't do coasting,' I heard my voice say.

The options felt as exhausted as I was. It was impossible to change course, to go back, there was only one way forward.

I bought a one-way ticket at Oxford railway station. I returned the way I came.

That Christmas I bought the Port from Victoria Wine. My Dad, to his credit didn't say anything until Boxing Day.

'We seem to have produced a van driver who reads *The Times*,' he observed.

I found work as a van driver, delivering blood packs to hospitals in the Leeds NHS area. I scanned the paper in my breaks.

Finally I negotiated my way in to York University. They credited my time at Oxford to admit me to their political science degree starting in the second year.

The rest is history.

It seemed a lifetime later when I spoke to C about how this story contemporaneously unfolded.

Now he was living by the coast, in Cornwall. I repeated the maxim that I have always done the best I can at the time with the information available at the time.

What did I want ? Confirmation, absolution?

The Clash were playing on the radio in the background. I remembered the song from the Orange Tree juke box

He looked at me and listened in silence. I thought I detected the trace of a smile.

Michaelmas 2018

Capital Code

To me it seemed like a lot of money. To him it didn't. Obviously.

The estate agent swivelled round in his chair. When he came full circle he put his hands behind his neck in what I assumed he'd read was a power pose and said

'59K? What kind of wardrobe are you looking for?'

It wasn't common then to refer to a thousand as K. It wasn't good manners but it was common to laugh at people who walked into estate agents in Richmond after the Big Bang and ask to see a selection of houses available for £59, 000.

I took a bus counter clockwise along the inner south circular. With each stop I gained a thousand pounds. By the end of the line that was an extra bedroom, at a stretch an overlooked balcony.

I had worked my way through practical chapters of Raban's London handbook *Soft City*. No pattern a clock would follow, Wimbledon, Highgate, Richmond, The book was based on districts, *soi-disant* London villages not post codes. Dulwich village was listed as SE22. That was the code the agent gave me.

On the first morning in my new home I rang to arrange the insurance. I could hear another chair swivel in a call centre far away.

'The side of the street you live on is SE15.'

The insurance rate was double. I called into the estate agent to let them know they had given me the wrong post code.

'Thanks,' he said, 'let me know if there is anything else we can do for you.'

4 Sided Bay

The bay is so enclosed the sea could feel grateful to be let in.

From land it is reached by descending from the cliff above by a single path. People coming up stand to one side as you are coming down. You smile to each other as if you know a secret. By sea a small craft could approach and beach itself on the pebbles. There is nothing human here, no surfing shack or café to build smoothies. At frequent intervals waves polish the pebbles. It sounds like those machines insomniacs can buy to place next to their bed.

Don't swim out too far, leave the place as you find it, arrive at first light, return before dark, otherwise do as you like.

The deed is done

I managed from 1957 to 2003. Then it came to me in a flash. You can do something about it, be the change.

I had spent some time in practice and online studying coaching. Although the occasional maxim may sound somewhat Christmas crackerish, it felt right to me. 'If you do what you always do, you'll get what you always have.' You don't have to do the same thing forever, change something that no longer works for you, for example your name.

I had lived with it long enough. I wanted a positive, simple change, respecting my past, works in the present, would last as far into the future as I could see.

In the solicitor's office the deed poll was composed. 'Do you want to think about it?' asked the solicitor. I already have, I replied.

I emerged with my new name. Same me but with forward movement. Renewing documents, renewing a given was a form of decluttering. Why hadn't I done it before?

I had a similar experience when I sold my house in York. An idea formulating for a long time, longer than you know, then action. It's time.

As I replaced the telephone receiver after calling the estate agent it started immediately. The house to the right was derelict, the house to the left overwhelmed me with noise, the loft above, the undercroft below were full. All I did was sit in the south facing yard. Can you do that forever?

I recycled things I had thought essential, things I never knew I had, things I felt I couldn't do without, why did I have them in the first place? 10% of my vinyl collection survived, I listened 90% more, surfaces surfaced.

At the end of the day I sat on the steps watching the sun set.

I showed people round the house. Why are you selling, where are you going?

I don't know, I said. People didn't like it. Why don't you know? It was so unsettling to so many I lost X% of the market price. You can't put figures on everything.

The last morning there I fastened my remaining cooking utensils to my bicycle handlebars and cycled away along the river bank. A journey without maps, a journey without a destination? A journey. /

YE 811531

CERTIFICATE OF BIRTH

Name and Surname	JOHN FRANCIS FAGAN
Sex	Boy
Date of Birth	Sixth March 1957
Place of Birth — Registration District	LEEDS
Place of Birth — Sub-district	ST. MARY'S

I, A. W. RICKETTS, Registrar of Births and Deaths for the Sub-district of ST. MARY'S do hereby certify that the above particulars have been compiled from an entry in a register in my custody.

Witness my hand this 30th day of March 1957.

CAUTION:—Any person who (1) falsifies any of the particulars on this certificate, or (2) uses a falsified certificate as true, knowing it to be false, is liable to prosecution.

A. W. Ricketts
Registrar of Births and Deaths

MVPD/178

THIS DEED is made on the 4th day of February 2003 by me JOHN FRANCIS TERENCE KING formerly called JOHN FRANCIS FAGAN of 10 Kyme Street York YO1 6HG a citizen of the United Kingdom by birth.

1. I, for and on behalf of myself wholly renounce, relinquish and abandon the use of my former name of JOHN FRANCIS FAGAN and in place of it assume from today the name of JOHN FRANCIS TERENCE KING so that I will from today be called known and distinguished not by my former name of JOHN FRANCIS FAGAN but by my assumed name of JOHN FRANCIS TERENCE KING.

2. I shall at all times from today in all records, deeds and writings and in all proceedings, dealings and transactions, private as well as public, and on all occasions use and sign the name of JOHN FRANCIS TERENCE KING as my name in place of and in substitution for my former name of JOHN FRANCIS FAGAN.

3. I therefore expressly authorise and request all persons at all times from today to designate and address me by my assumed name of JOHN FRANCIS TERENCE KING.

SIGNED AS A DEED by the above named)
JOHN FRANCIS TERENCE KING)   *J. F. King*
Formerly JOHN FRANCIS FAGAN)   *J. F. Fagan*
in the presence of)

P. M. Roberts-Garland
P. M. ROBERTS-GARLAND
SENTINEL HOUSE
PENSHOLME GREEN
YORK YO1 7PP

We hereby certify that this is a true copy of the original.
Ware & Kay
WARE & KAY, Solicitors, York

Relativity

I've always had a different view of time to CZ.

It isn't that his is more precious than mine and we both have the same amount of it. It is simply an alternative view.

Lunch wasn't on him only it was his turn to pay.

The waiter said 'I'll bring you the bill and you can pay over there. No problem.'

'I'm glad' replied CZ. He elaborated 'that there isn't a problem.'

The waiter was momentarily off balance. I was relieved he wasn't palming a full tray of drinks the way they do in American films.

A quantity of time seemed to pass before the bill was presented.

'No problem,' said the waiter.

'Don't' I said to CZ.

We walked over to the counter where the bill accepting machine worked.

'The machine is a bit slow today,' said the man feeding credit cards into the machine.

'No problem,' said CZ. You'd have to know him as well as I do to know the accompanying smile was devoid of humour. Or have the time.

Eventually the machine read the card. The man handed the card back to CZ.

'Thank you,' he said. 'Enjoy your day.'

'No problem,' said CZ.

We made it back to the street in time.

Check Off

Talking for a living is hard.

At the end of a day of 1:1 language training there are no words.

I am supposed to recognize low and high points in energy levels, why didn't I learn to do it for myself?

It was the lowest time in the week, in the day, in the hour but I thought I could make it before everything closed down.

The check out worker had a name badge on but I was scanned out. T, Trevor, Terry?

'How is your day, are you looking forward to the weekend, anything nice planned?'

I stared back at him in silence. I'm tired, you are too no doubt, who is the training manual spiel for?

I packed my stuff in my *One Planet York* bag and sloped on. I never looked back. The words 'enjoy your weekend' fell in the aisle.

I practised my apology all night. 'I'm most terribly sorry. Low time. Rude of me.' I could expand this to 'I'm not really like that, you know what customer facing roles are like, how was your weekend T?' Did he even have one?

Monday, same time, it was difficult to contrive to stay in that checkout line. I only bought one item and the store manager was agitated I wasn't in the 'four items or fewer' lane. When I made it to Trev he said ' how is your day, sir, are you looking forward to the week, anything nice planned?'

I said ' I'm most terribly sorry.'

I didn't plan my retirement at the time it happened. I'm at the store at a different time now. All the checkouts were automated. I don't know happened to Trev.

F for Fortitude

I knew the knock on the door would come.

I didn't know it would be 4 that morning.

From being asleep to in the car was 12 minutes.

We set off for the hospice. At this stage we had been there on a daily basis, one of the family always there day and night. This visit was different. This was it.

F was the last member of my immediate family alive. When she was diagnosed with cancer a year ago there wasn't a visible difference. She was very brave. Months later the situation was totally undeniable. I told her not to go but she never did listen to me.

It was Autumn by the time we arrived at the hospice. I don't know why it was the most fitting season.

We talked to the lead nurse. F will be gone in a few hours, she said. I was pleased she didn't use expressions like 'pass away.'

The nurse had seen it all before. Her prognosis was uncannily accurate.

I have seen people, close people, dying before. It is a deep privilege to be actually in the room at the moment of death. We all sat round the bed. We said goodbye, thank you, smiled, cried.

The last breath was taken.

In the October air of the north London afternoon I wanted a cup of tea. I wanted to tell people on the street that I'd awoken at 4am and hit the road at 4.12. That's why I imagined I looked like I did. Perhaps they wouldn't understand, they would have their own things to think upon.

There would be time for tea when we reached home.

Live in Leeds

Eavesdropping is wrong. I don't do it, never have.

Hearing speech without hearing words? Categorically different.

It wasn't every night, perhaps two, three, occasional night music.

I went to bed early in those days and slept. Next thing I knew it was morning, Weetabix, another day. It was a pre-day, new kind of sound, this sound without words.

'Goodnight mum, goodnight dad, God bless,' a late childhood routine. Routine can be good, send you to sleep.

The evenings I heard the sound were Sunday.

After tea, we sat in the front room. The front room was at the front of the house. It was always there but we were only in it on Sundays. Mum played the Schiedmayer. She was as upright as the piano.

Chopin, Beethoven, Mendelssohn, the song without words. After I retired for the evening the music stopped and I heard it. It wasn't murmuring, it wasn't a row, but to my ears it wasn't music. There was an unease in the speech, something not right, something disturbing, undefined.

At first the two voices were even in turn, tone, time. Then – unusually - my mother was speaking more with my Dad injecting one word, rhythmic, reassuring, repetitive. I never heard what that word was.

Whatever they were talking about it wasn't good. It was about something deep, buried, something that should have gone but hadn't and could come back.

It was the first time I knew that the world wasn't entirely alright, our place in it wasn't totally settled, that night wasn't an advisable time to be awake.

The voices ceased, I went to sleep, then it was Monday.

The weeks had their own rhythm, I liked it that way. The spin of the Hotpoint on Monday, haddock and chips on Friday, comedy shows on the BBC on Saturday, the sound of laughter. Then Sunday. Chopin, Beethoven, Mendelssohn, the sound, the wordless non-music floating up the stairs.

Sometimes the set list changed – the classics interspersed with ragtime, music hall, vocal arrangements, light positive words set to music – '*Let the Great Big World Keep Turning*', '*A Nightingale Sang in Berkeley Square,*' '*The Harry Lime Theme.*'

My mother could entertain light music too in her classical way.

Sundays were special then, not a positive or negative day in itself but not like the six others. Maybe that was it. The way my Dad parked the van on the street stopping play of the other kids asphalt street cricket when we came back from church, called in for dinner at 1pm, the long afternoons before the music after tea. Shops dark, choice of *World at War* or *Forsyte Saga* on the TV channels, the windows closed despite the smoke from my Dad's *Embassy*.

Midsummer meant seaside holidays. I loved the sea and sand. But that summer on the beaches of Devon and Dorset my Mum disappeared for three days. That's nearly 40% of the holiday.

'Where's mum?' I asked Dad. We were on the beach having fun but not so much I hadn't noticed her absence.

'Brussels,' said Dad

I looked at him for a long time before I decided not to pursue things. That evening my Dad showed me a picture postcard of the Brussels atomium.

'Mum is in Brussels, Belgium, abroad, at a relative's funeral. She'll be back tomorrow.'

Mum came back but she wasn't really there for the rest of the holiday.

'Who do – did, you – we – know – in Brussels, Belgium, mum?' I asked.

The names she listed back were unfamiliar in sound – Waldemar, Helga, Berbel, Willi.

If you asked a question it was answered, if you asked a supplementary it was answered. There was no evasion but that wasn't the point. You learned not to ask any more. It seemed to cause pain.

I was too old at this stage to continually respond to every answer I was given with another 'why.' I was old enough to detect that the answers merely led to more gaps, that there were layers beneath every story, the episodes were sudden rather than evolutionary, that we were a construct.

At University I sat up late with my friends discussing the tree in the forest anthropy. Pubs in 1976 closed at 1030pm. The college didn't admit girls. There was nothing better than getting epistemological at midnight.

-A tree falls in a snowy forest in the middle of the night; how do you know it makes a sound? Once I wondered if my Mum and Dad still had their conversation on those Sunday nights, if I would ever know the lyrics to that song.

University didn't lead to a glittering prize, it didn't immediately lead to anything. I returned home with no job. Everything had changed, everything had stayed the same. The situations vacant column carried an ad for the civil service. The forms had boxes to fill in on the background of both parents, where were they born, where were their parents born.

My Dad had done everything in his power to lead me to a professional work. Why didn't he want me to fill in this form, take an opportunity to join? Why leave boxes blank, silence on the page?

'Do you want me to get this job or don't you?' I had never spoken sharply to my Dad before, I was unnerved by my own noise.

Finally the answer was written down, there on the form. My mother Elsie was born Ilse Hölzelmacher in Vienna, 1928.

It was a beginning. Yes, I got the job but I moonlighted on another, the job of excavating my mother's genealogy. The job was part time, unpaid though not unrewarding. Unlike my other jobs I never finished it. The pattern continued until my Mum died, questions answered if you asked them, silence isn't evasion but if you want more you have to learn how to find it yourself.

At University I began studying history. By 1978, at a Phyrric personal cost to myself I negotiated a manoeuvre from medieval English history, of kings and 'great men', of irrelevance, to modern European history, of people and states, to relevance.

It was decades later before I detected a theme in what I had studied, where I had worked. Studying c20th European history and politics, library work in the information centres of the Foreign Office, the BBC, Chatham House, teaching work with students from all over the continent. Was it all a practical lesson, in history, in us, the construct?

My moonlighting job eventually revealed my mother's brother Alfons was born in Vienna district II 8 November 1930 and deported to Auschwitz 23 October 1944.

I was studying the history I was connected to, a history that could never be repeated, finding an answer to a question that could only be asked once.

Sunday is special today as all days are, time passes, time you are only given once. There are 100 channels on TV.

Earlier this century I was sitting in the car outside a synagogue. Last century I didn't properly knew what a synagogue was. On arrival in England in 1939 my mother was adopted by a Church of England vicar, later married a Catholic. On census forms I believe I tick 'No Religion.' What was I doing sitting outside a synagogue?

I was never a successful joiner of clubs – Marx had a point 'never join clubs that would have you as a member'. When there was no one left alive to ask I joined an organisation called Second Generation Network. It's all in the name, a network for the generation descended from first generation Holocaust survivors or refugees from Nazi occupied Europe.

The first meeting I planned to attend was in Roundhay, the suburb in north Leeds where my Mum and Dad were married.

I looked at the Star on the wall, what had this to do with me, it would be more fun to return home and watch telly.

I was about to select reverse gear when there was a tap on the windscreen.

I wound down the side window.

A woman smiled while reciting a list with an interrogative but friendly intonation: 'So where were your family – Auschwitz Birkenau, Theresienstadt, Buchenwald, Mauthausen...?'

What reply could be possible? Was this a code, an admission test? Should I essay a counter list – 'Le Touquet, Nice, Copenhagen...' Fortunately I had given up facetiousness in 1978. I remembered the sound of silence.

I opened the car door.

It seemed rude not to join. You could always leave if you didn't fit in.

When I arrived home there was a census form to complete. The box marked nationality had an 'other' option. The answer was obvious- 'British European.'

 /2g editorial

Different Trains

I knew, she knew.

My mother's life was coming to an end.

When she was gone the answers would go with her.

I'd already discovered facts in an international tracing service but the file wouldn't close. The time was now, ask my mum the right questions, the ones I thought she wanted me to.

I'd frame it with due sensitivity, how about -

'Mum, why did you get to the station and onto the train but Uncle Alfons didn't?'

I pictured the scene with what I already knew. My mum at Vienna main station, 1939. Her parents had collated papers with sufficient efficiency to satisfy the then authorities in Vienna, the point of departure and in England, where the new life could begin. I see a steam engine, a whirl of noise and smoke, the children only carriages leave the platform of forlorn adult waves

It is a before and after moment.

Mum, what was your life like in Vienna, school, home, music? I understood there were three children in the Hölzelmacher family, my mum, Ilse, her sister Isobel and their brother Alfons. Ilse was on the train. If she hadn't been I wouldn't exist so I wouldn't be able to type this. Isobel must have been otherwise she couldn't have gone to live in Cornwall, Alfons wasn't.

I asked the Austrian Embassy in London what happened to Alfons Hölzelmacher? I had a letter back return of post -

> Herr Alfons Hölzelmacher, born Wien district II 8 November 1930 deported to Auschwitz 23 October 1944.

I was working on reframing the question, the tone, the tenses. My mother had the grace to complete the task for me.

'There was never a day when I didn't think of Alfons.'

The past is the past, don't mess with answers.

See also Eurostars in Funky / Guy 2012

Memories of the Future

Timeline

'..If we see time as eternally present that at any given moment we are seeing only a cross-section of ourselves .. we can transcend our suffering and have no need to hurt or have conflict with other people..'

J B Priestley, *Time and the Conways* 1937. NT 2009, BBC radio: 1994, 2014

T F Fagan

born Hull 30 October 1924 + Leeds (Calverley), All Souls 1985

My father grew up in Wakefield.

During World War II, he served in ARP, Home Guard and with the Royal Engineers in France and Germany.

/Normandy campaign medal

After studying for his HND he worked at *English Electric* Bradford until his retirement.

He worked on *Lightning* aircraft and *Deltic* locomotives.

/Deltic at NRM, Science Museum York

Ilse Hölzelmacher / Lambert Smith / Fagan

My mother was born in Vienna 26 August 1928 + Leeds (Ilkley), HMD 2011

She was adopted into the **Lambert Smith** (formerly *Spiegelhalter*) family on arrival in England by Kindertransport, 1939.

Elsie went to school in Bridlington and *Whitby, Eskdale* and trained as SRN at Leeds General Infirmary. Following her retirement as district nurse based in Calverley, Leeds she studied for an Open University BA degree.

/HLS Photography: Whitby Pannett

An excellent pianist she also volunteered as church organist at *St Joseph* and St Wilfred churches near Leeds and travelled widely in Europe and North America.

Mum's 80th birthday at Stokesley, N Yorkshire 2008

My Mum and Dad bought their first house in Roundhay Leeds/

/My sister **Margaret** was born there, + Hampstead, London 3.10.2013

*Touring in Le Touquet, Pas-de-Calais 1967,
walking in Cotterdale, Wensleydale 1975 with Mum and Dad/*

John Francis Terence King (Fagan<2003)

Born Leeds 6 March 1957

1962

Primary school at *St Joseph*, Pudsey, Leeds.

Headmaster: Mr Harwood

1968

School at Cardinal Hinsley Grammar, Bradford.

Form master Mr Brodie

Music master, organist, orchestra conductor and arranger Mr Haynes

1964 Wilson government 1, 1974 2

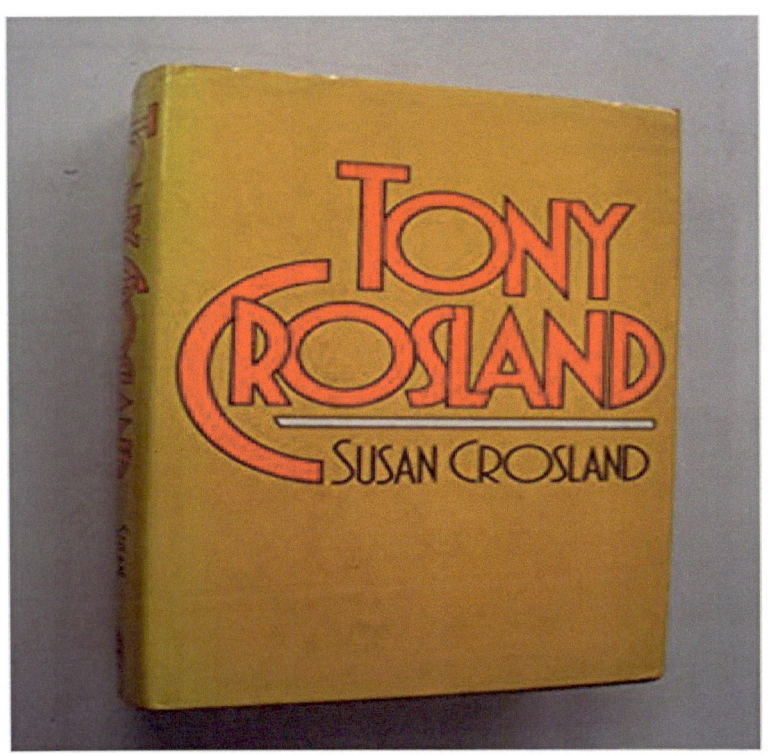

1969 Foundation of Open University

1968

Student / anti-war / civil rights demonstrations in Berlin, Paris, London, Prague, Memphis - M L King+

RFK Funeral train NY to Washington DC

1969

US Apollo mission 11

/poster, York City Screen, 2018.

At school we watched a live relay of the lunar landing with science master Dr Howard.

1969 Beatles last live public performance, London

Soft Machine live at BBC Proms

1970

Roxy Music formation

1973

Sixth form studies, A/S and Oxford University entrance examinations under direction of Mr J Canning, headmaster Mr W E Earnshaw.

Independent music study at *Yorkshire College of Music, Headingley, Leeds6./*

1975

/Powell novel sequence, A Dance to the Music of Time subsequently adapted for TV 1997. The radio productions 1979, 2008 led to a continuing interest in audio drama.

EEC referendum 1975, EU referendum 2016

'gap year' - driver for Leeds NHS area hospital service

YHA warden, High Close, Grasmere, Lake District /

French studies course, Nice university then *Inter-rail tour of Europe* /

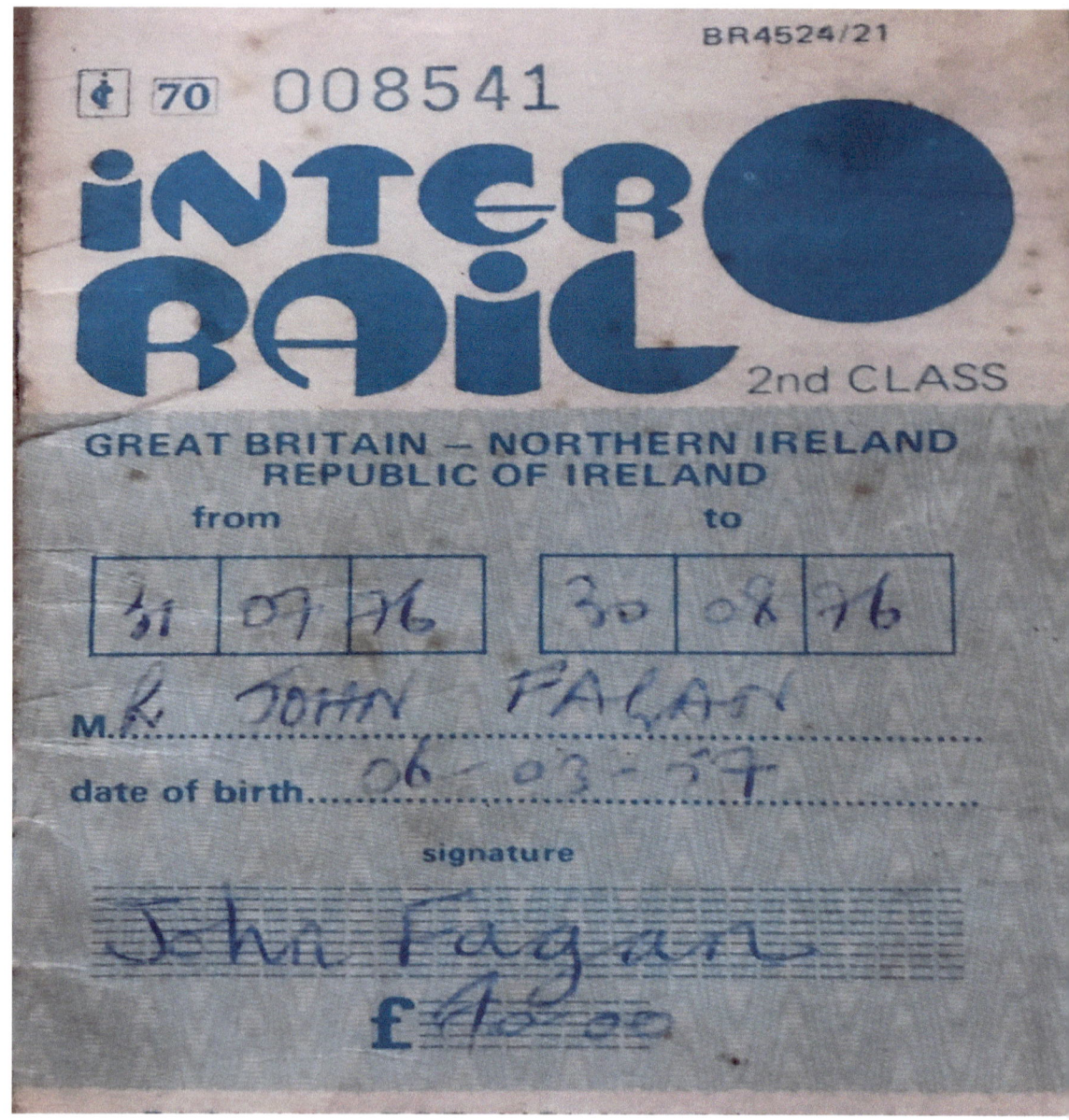

1976

Matriculation. *Pembroke College Oxford*

7.10.1976

1978 *University of York,* supervisors Drs Alderman, Cerny, Lister.

1980 BA Hons

University contemporaries include

P Ashworth, M Bennett, B Bhutto, H Enfield, H Fielding, D Goodhart, W Goymer, G Hadfield, C Parsons, C Pratt, M Saban, C Risner, J Warren

1977 death of Maria Callas

Rock against Racism, The Clash, central and east London 1978

1981

Move from Leeds to London – Wimbledon, Highgate, Richmond, Dulwich

Work at FCO, BBC, *RIIA Chatham House, Independent study at Goethe institute, London SW7*

The Royal Institute of ... Affairs

March–April 1990
GOETHE
INSTITUT
LONDON

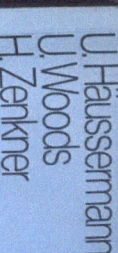

RICHARD STRAUSS
VIER LETZTE LIEDER
4 SONGS / QUATRE DERNIERS LIEDER
KIRI TE KANAWA
... (PIANO)
DECCA

U. Häussermann
U. Woods
H. Zenkner

Sprachkurs Deutsch 2

Diesterweg
ÖBV
Sauerländer

1980 death of John Lennon
1985 Shoah / Lanzmann
1985 Live Aid

1985 Rainbow Warrior incident NZ

GREENPEACE

1987 death of Clement Attlee
1989 fall of Berlin Wall—

Deutsch-Britische Gesellschaft

Konigswinter

1989

MA *UCL* Library and information studies, supervisor Dr McIlwaine

Library, Chatham House 1991

/Library, Dubai 2017 ADL

Following the MA I set up the information service at the North Yorkshire European Community Office.

Here I contributed media presentations

(e.g. to BBC radio, York Evening Press, chambers of commerce, Rotary Club, University of York, and businesses including York Associates)

as the UK entered the European Single Market, New Year Day 1993.)

After gaining the CELTA at ILI in 1994 I began my career as a freelance trainer and contributed to professional publications as writer / editor.

2019

John F Fagan, MA
Information Officer

NYECO

**North Yorkshire European
Community Office Ltd**
2 Front Street, Acomb, York. YO2 3BZ
Tel: (0904) 788592 Fax: (0904) 788593

John King International
Coaching, Writing

John F King

jftking1@gmail.com
www.johnkinginternational.eu

1990 Mandela walks to freedom

1991 John McCarthy released from Lebanon

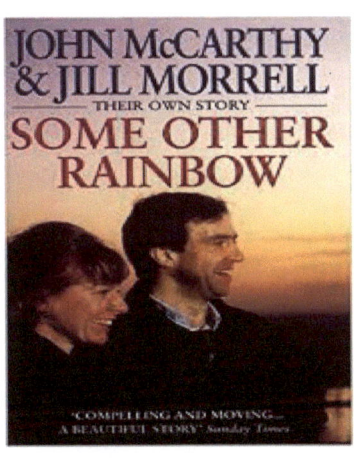

1992

Move from London to York *Bishophill/*

NYECO 1992 – 1994, including visit to *EP Brussels*

1994

York Associates, ELT 1994 -

1995 *Windows* GUI computers introduced at work and home

Certificate of Participation

We have the pleasure of confirming that

John F. King

participated in the 18th IATEFL BESIG Conference held on
11 - 13 November, 2005 at the International University of Monaco

2005 presentation at BESIG, IATEFL Monaco

1997 Blair Government 1

1999 The West Wing series 1, *The Wire* series 1 2002, *Borgen* series 1 2010, *House of Cards* 1990/ 2013

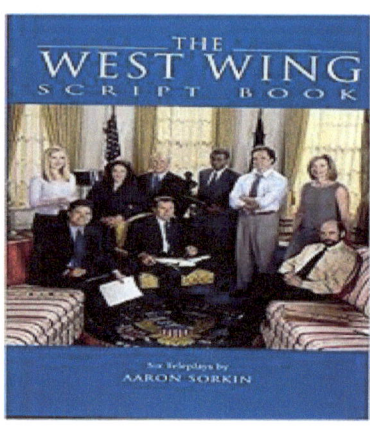

2001 9/11 Terror attacks in USA

2005 England regain the Ashes

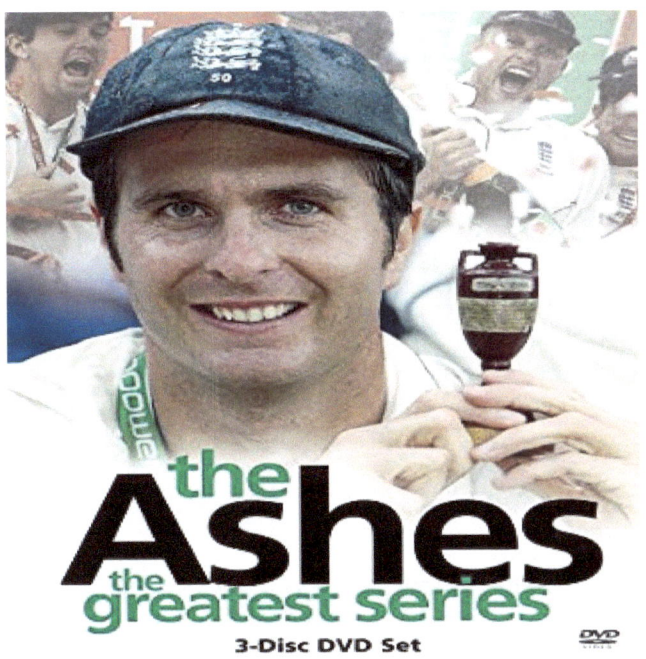

2009

Plays *Platform Free* performed at Script York, director Mark Smith, and *Smoke** (written with Alan Ram) at Script Factor

Platform Free produced by Walter Swan, director Ash Caton, *Ilkley Playhouse* 2014.

```
2009 Barack Obama wins Nobel Peace Prize
```

2011

David Hockney: *Arrival of Spring*, Saltaire.
& Tate Britain 2017, visited on my 60th birthday with ADL and AQM.

2014

Creative writing tutor as NHS volunteer, *Ilkley library*

Creative Writing Group leader, John King

Share your stories with writing group

BUDDING writers are invited to come along to a free Creative Writing Group hosted by Bradford District Care Trust's Champions Show the Way team at Ilkley Library.

Held every Wednesday from 1pm to 3pm, attendees will have the opportunity to put pen to paper and write a range of novels, short stories, letters to the newspaper, personal diary and/or blogs.

Bradford District Care Trust's Community Health Champion, John King, leads the group. He said: "It is great to hear people's stories – the angles, the styles, the experiences – everyone has their own way of working and writing and the space that they have in the group encourages that. Everyone in the group has been pleasan surprised at what they do and how they have veloped."

Just turn up at Ilkley brary by 1pm on Wed day afternoons, or 01274 321911 or e-r champions@bdct.nhs.u

2016

President Obama and The Rolling Stones, Cuban Easter

2016

To York *Bishopthorpe/*

/On Sustrans route 65 / Ebor Way midsummer 2018

Ebor way, Winter solstice

Memories of the Future, York Europe Publishing

www.johnkinginternational.eu

www.johnkinginternational.co.uk

supports-

-Memories of the Future

by J F King 2019.

Also by John F King at York Europe Publishing:

Wise Guy and other fables, 2008

ISBN 978-0-955851902

> **Wise Guy,** 2012, is also available as an eBook at
>
> Smashwords ISBN 9781476351735

*__Drama King__, 2010

ISBN 978-0-955851919

Funky / Guy and other micro-fiction, 2012

ISBN 978-0-955851964

Micro-Waves, 2012

ISBN 978-0-955851933

Vienna, Love, 2014

ISBN 978-0-955851971

Write Coach, 2014

ISBN 978-0-955851988

Write Coach II 2015

ISBN 978-0-9931306-1-8

A and E 2014

ISBN 978-0-955851995

Prog 2015

ISBN 978-0-9931306-0-1

What's Left 2016

ISBN 978-0-993106-2-5

Low – Rise 2016

ISBN 978-0-9931306-3-2

SW10 2017

ISBN 978-09931306-4-9

West End Story 2018

ISBN 978-0-993106-5-6

Nice People 2018

ISBN 978-0-99331306-6-3

Memories of the Future

/York Minster